better together*

* This book is best read together, grownup and kid.

 **akidsco.com**

a kids book about

a kids book about

SAFETY

by Soraya Sutherlin, CEM®

in partnership with JUDY

A Kids Co.
Editor Jennifer Goldstein
Designer Rick DeLucco
Creative Director Rick DeLucco
Studio Manager Kenya Feldes
Sales Director Melanie Wilkins
Head of Books Jennifer Goldstein
CEO and Founder Jelani Memory

DK
Senior Production Editor Jennifer Murray
Senior Production Controller Louise Minihane
Senior Acquisitions Editor Katy Flint
Acquisitions Project Editor Sara Forster
Managing Art Editor Vicky Short
Managing Director, Licensing Mark Searle

First American edition, 2025
Published in the United States by DK Publishing, 1745 Broadway, 20th Floor,
New York, NY 10019

First published in Great Britain in 2025 by
Dorling Kindersley Limited, 20 Vauxhall Bridge Road, London SW1V 2SA
A Penguin Random House Company

The authorised representative in the EEA is
Dorling Kindersley Verlag GmbH. Arnulfstr. 124, 80636 Munich, Germany

A catalog record for this book is available from the Library of Congress.
A CIP catalogue record for this book is available from the British Library.
ISBN: 978-0-2417-4337-9

DK books are available at special discounts when purchased in bulk for sales
promotions, premiums, fund-raising, or education use. For details, contact:
DK Publishing Special Markets, 1745 Broadway, 20th Floor, New York, NY 10019
SpecialSales@dk.com

Printed and bound in China
www.dk.com
akidsco.com

MIX
Paper | Supporting
responsible forestry
FSC™ C018179

This book was made with Forest
Stewardship Council™ certified
paper – one small step in DK's
commitment to a sustainable future.
Learn more at **www.dk.com/uk/
information/sustainability**

For the kiddos out there who will inspire their families to be safer and more prepared for emergencies.

To my inquisitive children, Lily, Andrew, and Grace, who keep me grounded and fill our lives with laughter. Never stop asking questions, even the tough ones.

Intro
for grownups

There are different kinds of emergencies that happen in our world. There are some that are small (like the everyday bumps and bruises), and there are some that are big. Life-changingly big. And whether it's the house fires we see on late-night news coverage or the hurricanes that blow away beach towns, there's one thing that you likely always say to yourself when you're watching: "This would never happen to me."

Though we hope they never do, we're more vulnerable to these types of disasters than we think. And while we can't always prevent things like storms or earthquakes from happening, we can ABSOLUTELY prepare our families for them. And that starts with making an emergency plan.

It's OK if you've never talked about an emergency plan with your kids before. And it's OK if you don't know where to begin. This book is here to help you do exactly that.

Have you ever thought about

WHAT YOU WOULD DO IF THE BUILDING YOU WERE IN CAUGHT ON FIRE?

Have you ever wondered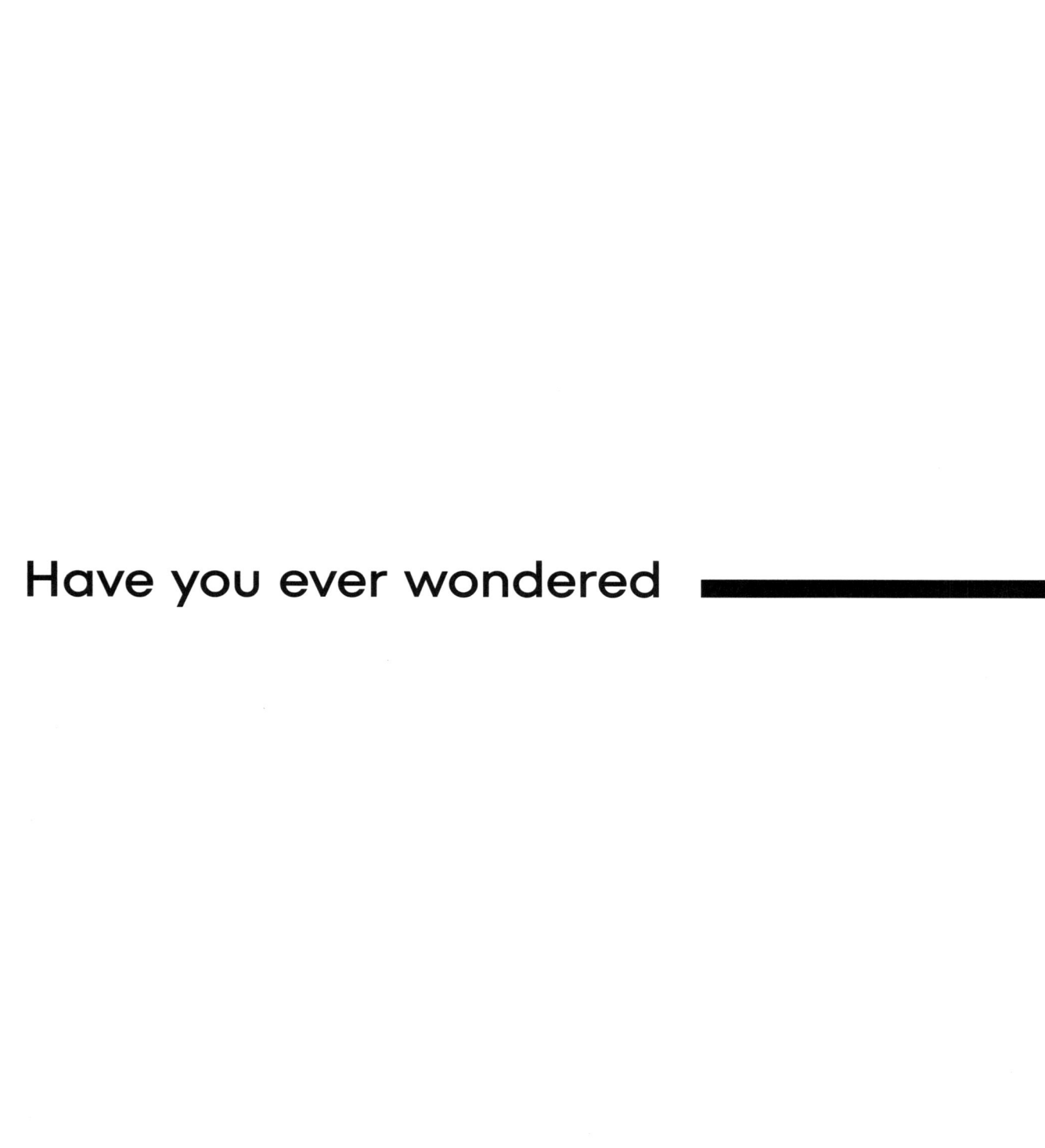

HOW TO STAY SAFE IF THERE WERE AN EARTHQUAKE?

Have you ever asked yourself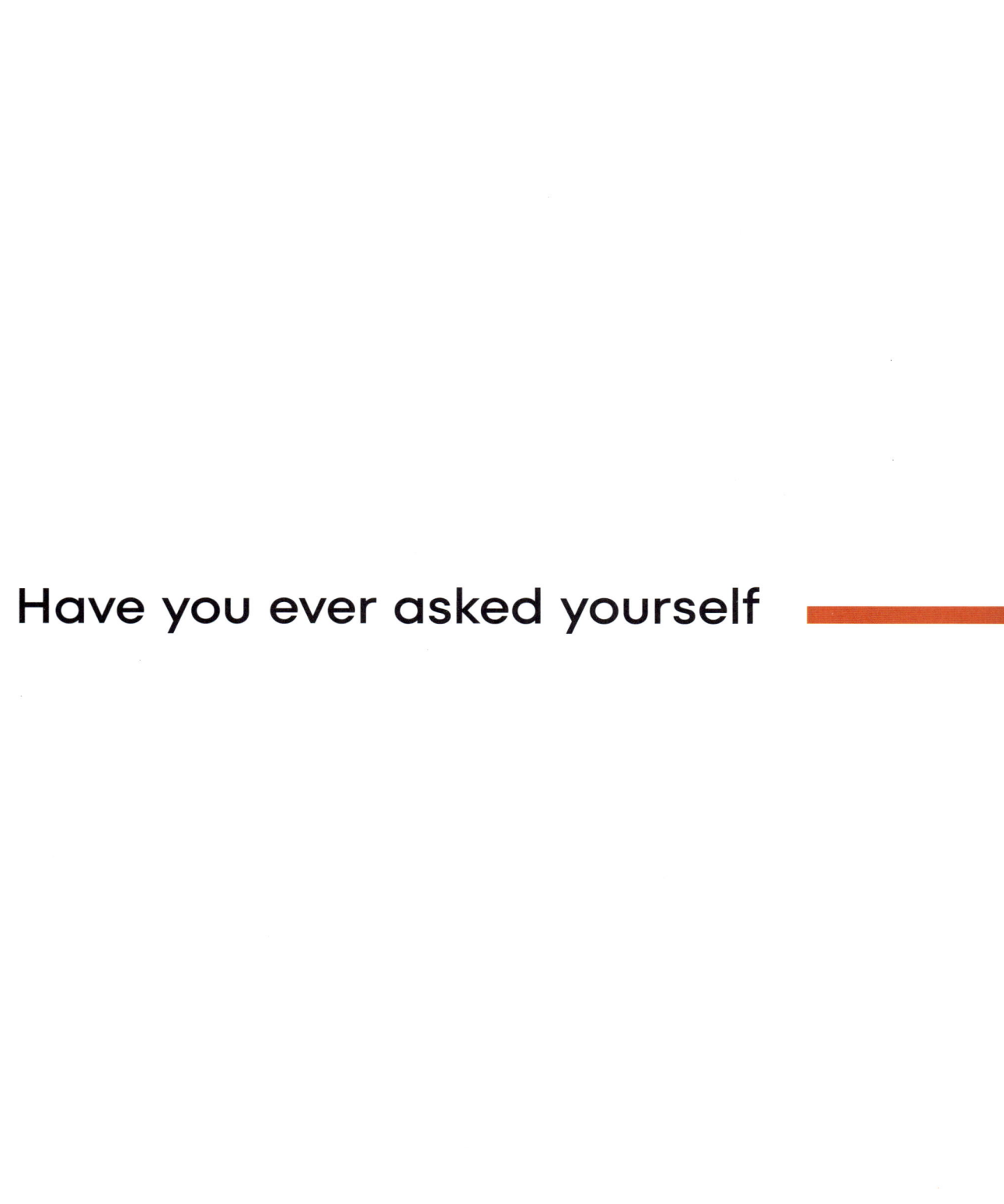

WHAT WOULD STOP WORKING IF YOUR POWER WENT OUT?

These might seem like silly questions, but they're actually really important.

They're not just important for the grownups in your life...

they're also really important for you to think about.

Yes, **YOU!** The kid.

Why?

Because dangerous things happen.

YUP, THEY DO.

 Sometimes fires start in places where they aren't supposed to.

 Earthquakes can shake the house in the middle of the night when everyone is asleep.

 We sometimes lose electricity when it is really cold, or really hot, outside.

And people can get hurt...

or even die.

So what can you do about it?

YOU CAN BE
PREP

ARED

But what does being prepared mean?

IT MEANS...

- ✅ Know what types of emergencies could happen near you.

- ✅ Know who your helpers would be if those emergencies actually happened.

- ✅ Know what tools you would need in an emergency situation.

- ✅ Make a plan.

- ✅ Practice your plan so you're ready.

STEP 01

This step is easy—we start by TALKING about emergencies.

Find time to talk with your family and ask each person to share different kinds of emergencies they think could happen.*

*Some of these emergencies could be natural disasters caused by the weather or earthquakes, and others may be due to the actions of people.

Here's a handy list of emergencies
you may have heard about:

FIRES 🔥

FLOODS 💧

EARTHQUAKES 🏠

TSUNAMIS 🌊

TORNADOES 🌪

HURRICANES 🌀

THUNDERSTORMS ⛈

POWER OUTAGES ⚡

Can you think of anything else?

STEP 02

Next, you can think about how you would get help if you were ever in one of those emergencies.

It's **OK** to stop and talk about it.

Let's think of a few possible helpers in your community.

Those could be:

TRUSTED NEIGHBORS

POLICE OFFICERS

TEACHERS

NURSES

FAMILY AND FRIENDS
FIREFIGHTERS
DOCTORS
COACHES

Can you think of anyone else?*

*Now remember, some people might not be safe for you. Make sure to talk about who is safe and who isn't with your family.

STEP 03

Have the tools you need.

We're not talking about things like shovels and hammers...**NO!**

We are talking about things that could be helpful in an emergency.

Some of these tools may be:

BANDAGES, FLASHLIGHTS, FIRST AID KITS, A RADIO, WHISTLES, OR...

LEARNING INFORMATION!

Like:

Knowing **WHERE TO GO** for help.

Knowing the **PHONE NUMBERS** to call, like **9 1 1**, and having a phone that is charged.

HAVING A GO BAG.

That's a bag you would take with you that has all the things you might need in case of an emergency.

PICK SOME ITEMS TO PUT IN YOUR GO BAG. Grownups should be in charge of things like flashlights and first aid kits...but it's important that kids gather tools that make them feel calm and safe, like a book, stuffed animal, or special toy.

Think about what tools you and your family will need and start working together to make your go bag!

STEP 04

Now it's time to make that plan.

Let's try making one together.

Your plan may look different, depending on what type of emergency you are making it for.

This example is about preparing in case of a house fire.

EMERGENCY HOUSE FIRE PLAN:

Look to make sure you have a working fire extinguisher* in your house that is not expired.

Sleep with your bedroom door closed. Doing so prevents the fire from spreading to rooms where people are sleeping.

*A fire extinguisher does exactly what it says—it extinguishes (or puts out) fires!

Make sure you have a smoke detector inside and outside of every bedroom, and on every level of your house.

Check all your smoke detectors and carbon monoxide detectors every month to make sure they work.*

And change their batteries twice a year.

*If they do, they'll make a really loud **BEEEEEP!**

*That's right, you definitely get to **YELL** if there's a fire.

Place a pair of old sneakers in your go bag so that if you need to get out of your house in the middle of the night, you'll have shoes for your feet!

Find 2 ways to get out of every room.*

Talk about how everyone can
(and will) get out.*

*Especially if they need extra help.

Choose a place to meet outside your house once you get out.*

*And make sure everyone else knows where that spot is too.

Practice meeting at that spot and count everyone who is there to make sure no one is missing!

It's important to stay put so your family will know you are safe.

If someone is missing, don't go back into danger.

Instead, tell the authorities, like firefighters and police, so they can rescue that person safely.*

*Firefighters can look scary when they are wearing their big jackets, boots, and helmet and carrying things like a hose or an axe. But they are there to help you. So don't hide! If you see or hear them, let them know where you are by calling out to them.

Take a moment.

You should be really
proud of yourself!

You've learned the basic
steps about how you can
save your life during
a fire emergency.

So what's next?

The goal is to make sure you **HAVE** a plan and that you actually **PRACTICE** that plan.

STEP 05

That leads us
to the final step:
practicing your plan
so you're ready.

Not just once,
but lots of times!

Here's an example of how to practice escaping a house fire:

Set a timer for 2 minutes...

and see if you're able to evacuate your home before the timer goes off.

Then, practice a few more times, trying different routes.

Please remember to find at least 2 possible routes out of every room and out of your house.

Sometimes that might mean using a window, so talk to your grownups about what you would do in that situation.

Having things like a throw ladder to help you safely escape may be something to discuss.

Practice

STOP, AND

DROP, ROLL,

so you are prepared if you or a family member's clothes catch on fire.

It may feel silly pretending
to get out of your house,
or to stop, drop, and roll
when the house isn't on fire.

But when you practice,
you prepare your body and mind
to act in case of an emergency.

Practicing improves your ability
to respond to emergency situations,
just like how practice helps improve
your learning in school, or your skills
on a sports team, or in band, or
ANYTHING!

Practicing can be inconvenient, uncomfortable, seem uncool, and may take up a Saturday afternoon.

But when a disaster or an emergency happens, like a flood, fire, or earthquake, it's important to feel confident and know what you would do before it happens.

Whether you know it or not,

YOU'RE PART OF A TEAM.

Your family, your friends, your school, your community—these are your helpers.

You all work together like a team to keep each other safe.

And **YOU** are a really important part of that team.

So use all of your senses.

If you...

FEEL IT.

HEAR IT.

SEE IT.

SMELL IT.

SENSE IT.

Tell someone.

Because your actions matter and you have more power than you know.

You could save a life—
maybe even your own.

So pay attention to
what's around you.

Take time every day
to notice what's
safe...

and what might
not be safe.

Knowing what could happen
and what to do if it does
makes you ready.

So remember:

you can help yourself
and the people around you
in an emergency if you...

- ✅ **PREPARE**

- ✅ **PRACTICE**

- ✅ **KNOW YOUR HELPERS**

- ✅ **USE YOUR TOOLS**

- ✅ **STAY CALM AND FOCUSED**

YOU CAN DO THIS!

EMERGENCIES WHERE I LIVE:

_____   _____

_____   _____

TOOLS I MIGHT NEED:

_____   _____

_____   _____

WHO CAN HELP?

_____   _____

_____   _____

2 PHONE NUMBERS I CAN CALL:

_____   _____

OUR OUTSIDE MEETING PLACE:

_____

_____

_____

Outro
for grownups

ow that you've finished this book, what's next? If you're a grownup reading this with your kid, it's important to remind them of 2 key things:

1. YES, these bad things can happen. But they don't happen to us every single day.

2. These types of emergencies can make us all feel really scared. (Yup, even the grownups.)

You set the tone from here on out. When you hear about things happening like a wildfire, a tornado, or even a medical emergency, take that as an opportunity to talk with your kid about your own emergency plan.

Get them involved! Ask **THEM** what they would do if they were ever in an emergency. And if they have questions and you don't have answers, look for them together. Because getting kids involved is getting them ready.

So start making safety a tradition in your house. The more you talk about it, the more prepared you can all be to survive a possible emergency.

About JUDY

Our mission is to help every family stay prepared.

With natural disasters happening more frequently and with bigger impact, having the right supplies and emergency plans is more important than ever. That's why we're dedicated to making preparation a household essential. If you're interested in learning more about emergency preparedness or getting an emergency kit of your own, please visit **JUDY.CO**.

Made to empower.

    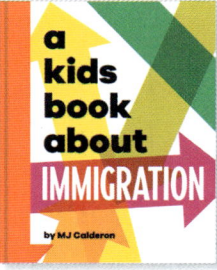

 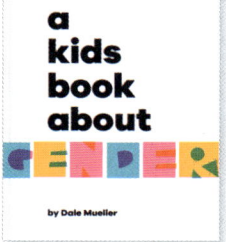 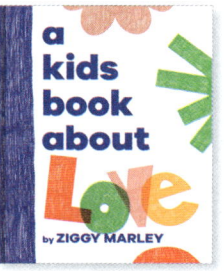 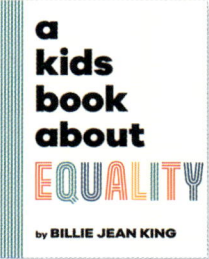 

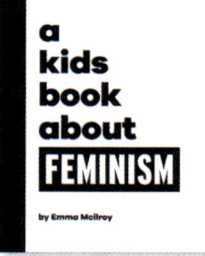 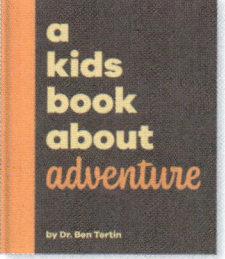